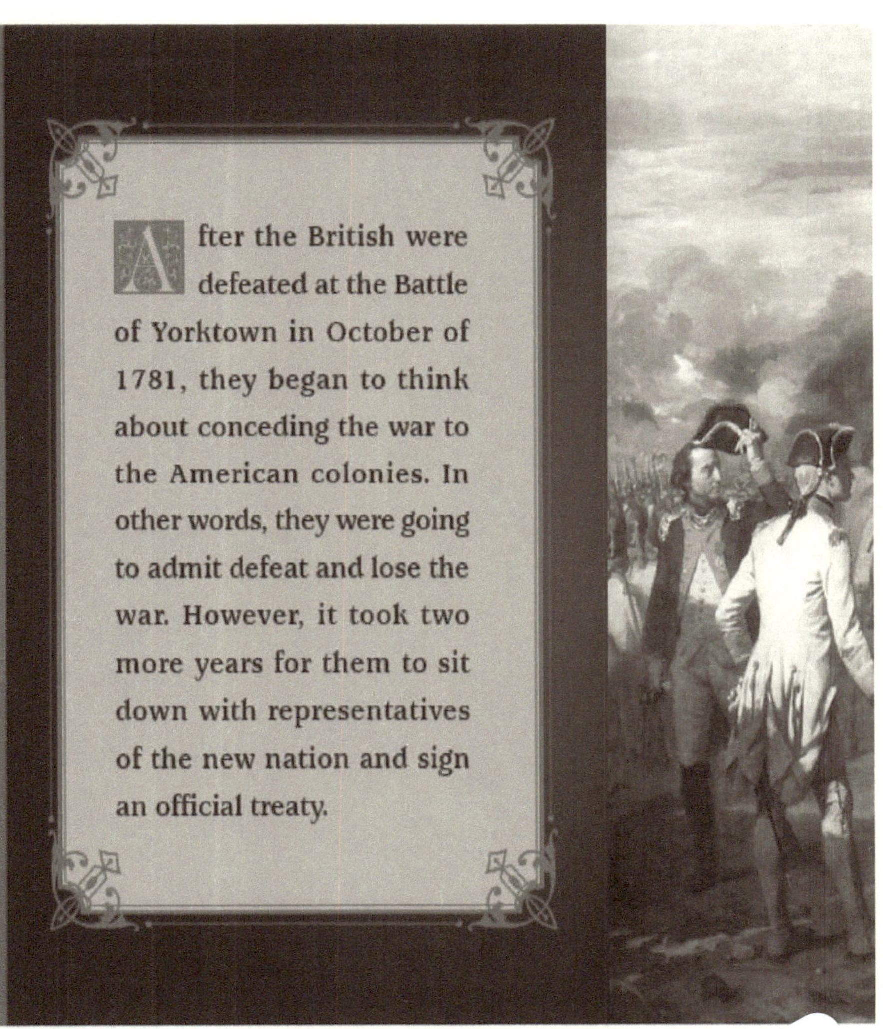

After the British were defeated at the Battle of Yorktown in October of 1781, they began to think about conceding the war to the American colonies. In other words, they were going to admit defeat and lose the war. However, it took two more years for them to sit down with representatives of the new nation and sign an official treaty.

SIGNING THE PRELIMINARY
TREATY OF PEACE AT PARIS

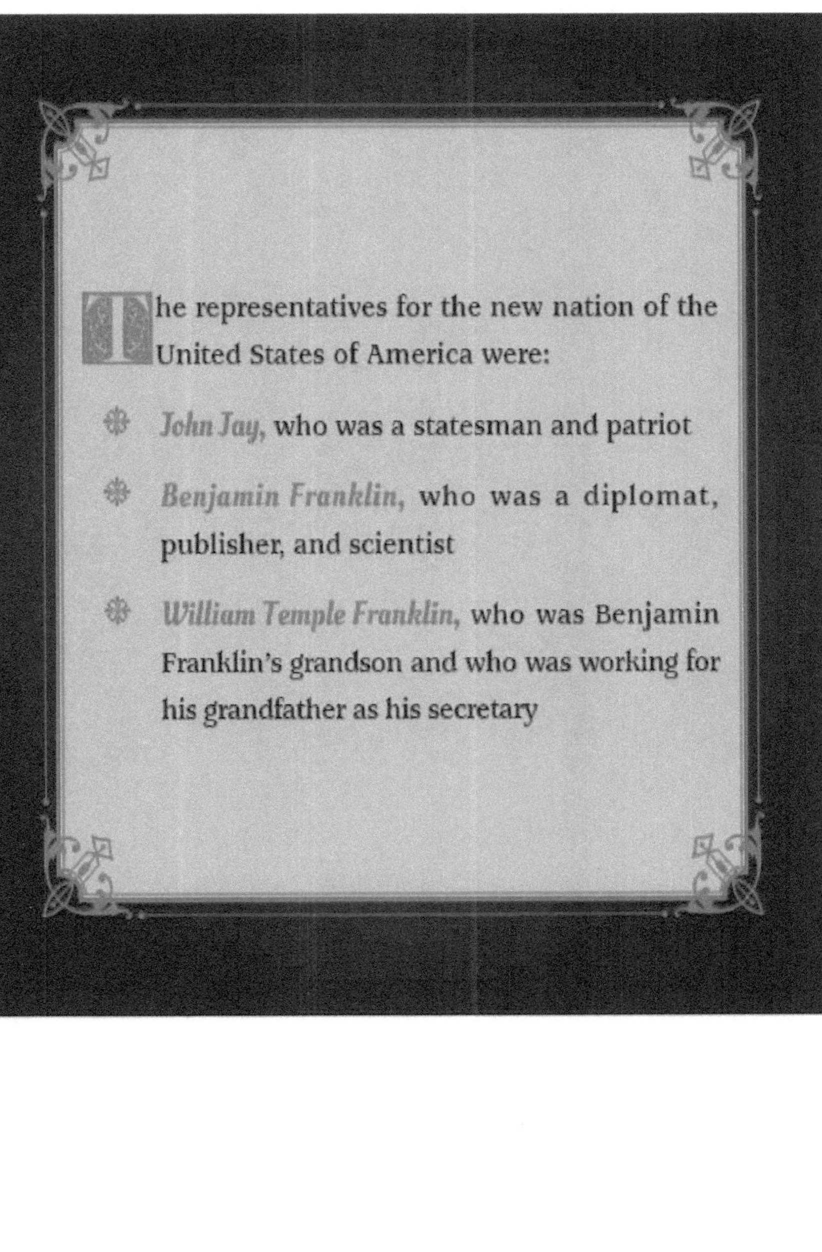

The representatives for the new nation of the United States of America were:

- *John Jay,* who was a statesman and patriot

- *Benjamin Franklin,* who was a diplomat, publisher, and scientist

- *William Temple Franklin,* who was Benjamin Franklin's grandson and who was working for his grandfather as his secretary

✤ *Henry Laurens,* who was an influential merchant from the South

RICHARD OSWALD

BRITISH COLONIES, 1763-1766

In addition to the agreements that Great Britain made with the new nation, there were separate agreements with the country of France and the country of Spain as well as with the Dutch Republic.

THE BEGINNING OF THE NEGOTIATIONS

The negotiations for the treaty had begun in the springtime in April of 1782 and they continued to go on throughout the summer months. Events came to a head in September. At that time, the French, who were represented by Vergennes, their Foreign Minister, came up with a plan that the United States didn't want, even though the French and the Americans were allies.

SIEGE OF GIBRALTAR AND
EXPLOSION OF 1782

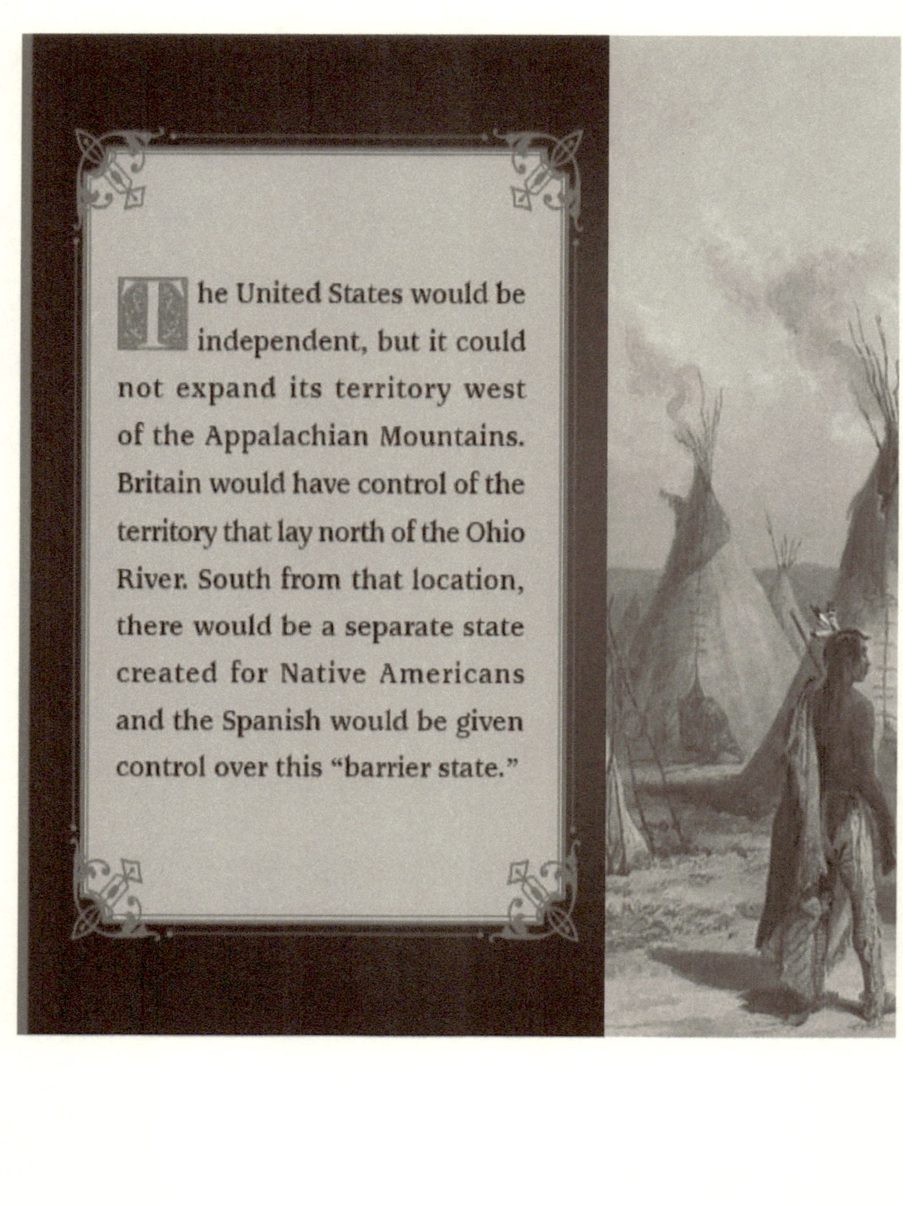

The United States would be independent, but it could not expand its territory west of the Appalachian Mountains. Britain would have control of the territory that lay north of the Ohio River. South from that location, there would be a separate state created for Native Americans and the Spanish would be given control over this "barrier state."

However, the Americans already knew that the new country would want to expand beyond the Appalachian Mountains.

WILLIAM PETTY, 2ND EARL OF SHELBURNE

Also, he believed that these negotiations would separate the United States and their ally France, since France and Great Britain had long been enemies.

THE TERMS OF THE AGREEMENT BETWEEN THE US AND BRITAIN

As negotiations continued directly with the British, the terms proposed were very favorable for the United States. The British eventually benefitted from these generous terms, since the United States became an ally and a very profitable trading partner as the growth of the new country exploded.

In addition to the king acknowledging that the United States was now a separate country and free from British rule, the new boundaries were specified as follows:

❄ The northern boundary between Canada and the United States was designated to be almost the same boundary as it is today. The new country would also have the right to fish off the coasts of Canada.

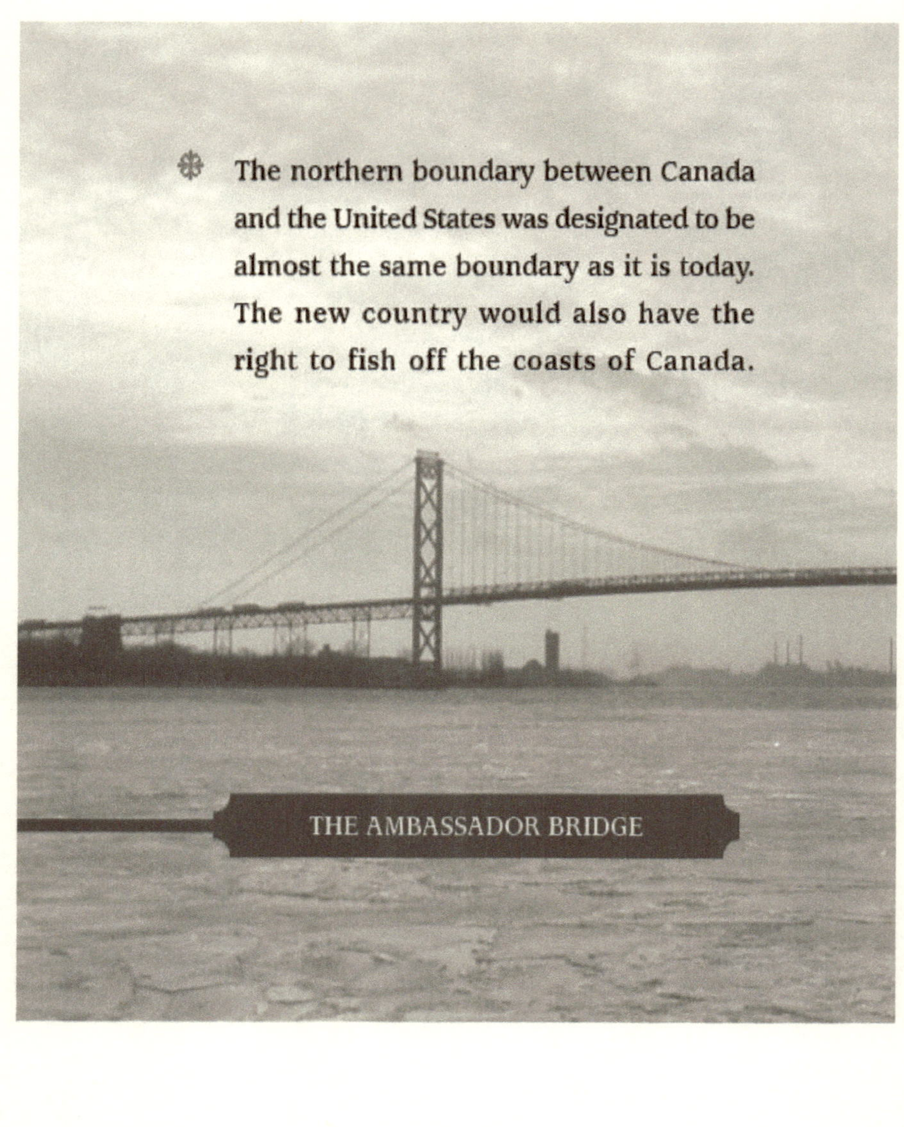

THE PEACE OF PARIS

Now that Great Britain was negotiating with the United States directly, the British had to negotiate with the US allies as well. There were separate agreements for each.

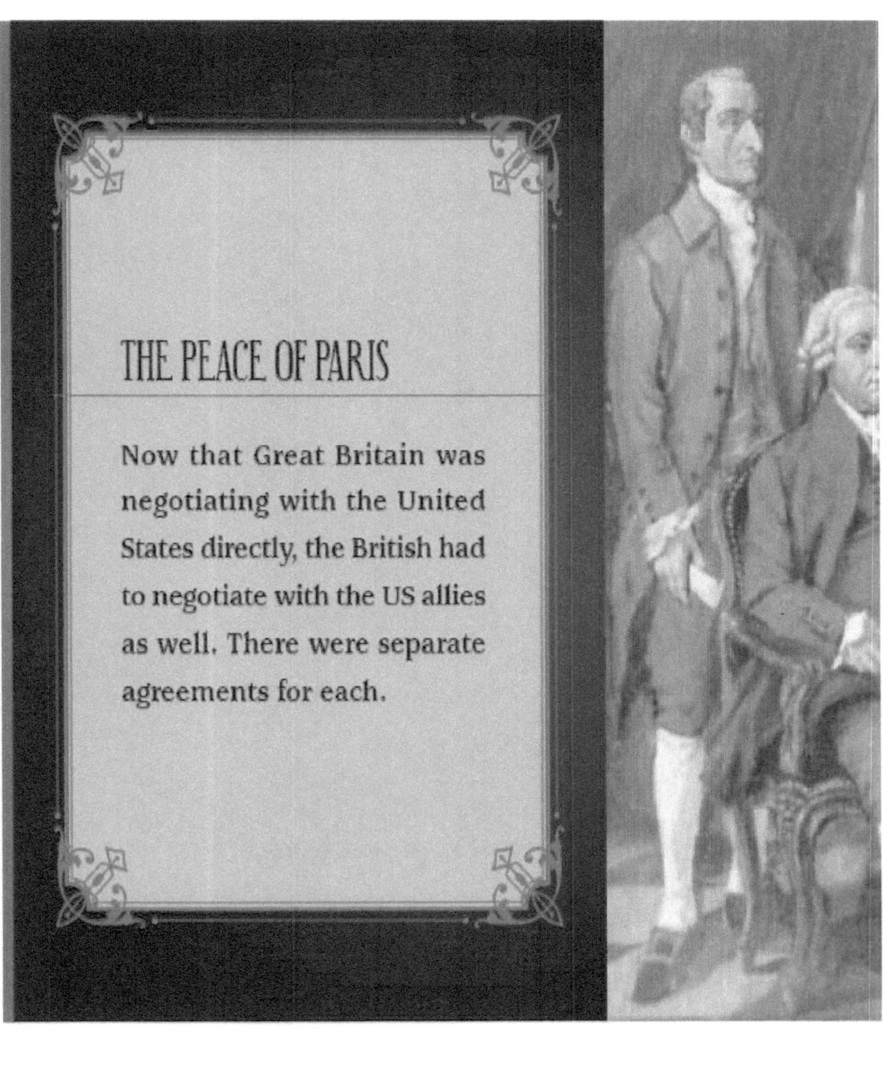

MINORCA SPAIN TODAY

FRANCE

France and England had been seizing each other's lands so under the treaty they exchanged lands that had been seized.

THE DUTCH REPUBLIC

Britain returned lands that they had seized in the East Indies in 1781. In exchange, they wanted to trade with the East Indies since the Dutch would now have power over it.

CONSEQUENCES OF THE TREATY

The Treaty extended the boundaries of the United States and the population began to grow and move west. As this occurred, new, profitable markets were opened up for trade. These markets were lucrative for the merchants of Britain and they could gain from them without any costs to the military since they would not continue to fight.

The lands known as Vermont were included in the United States because the government of New York State said that Vermont was within its boundaries.

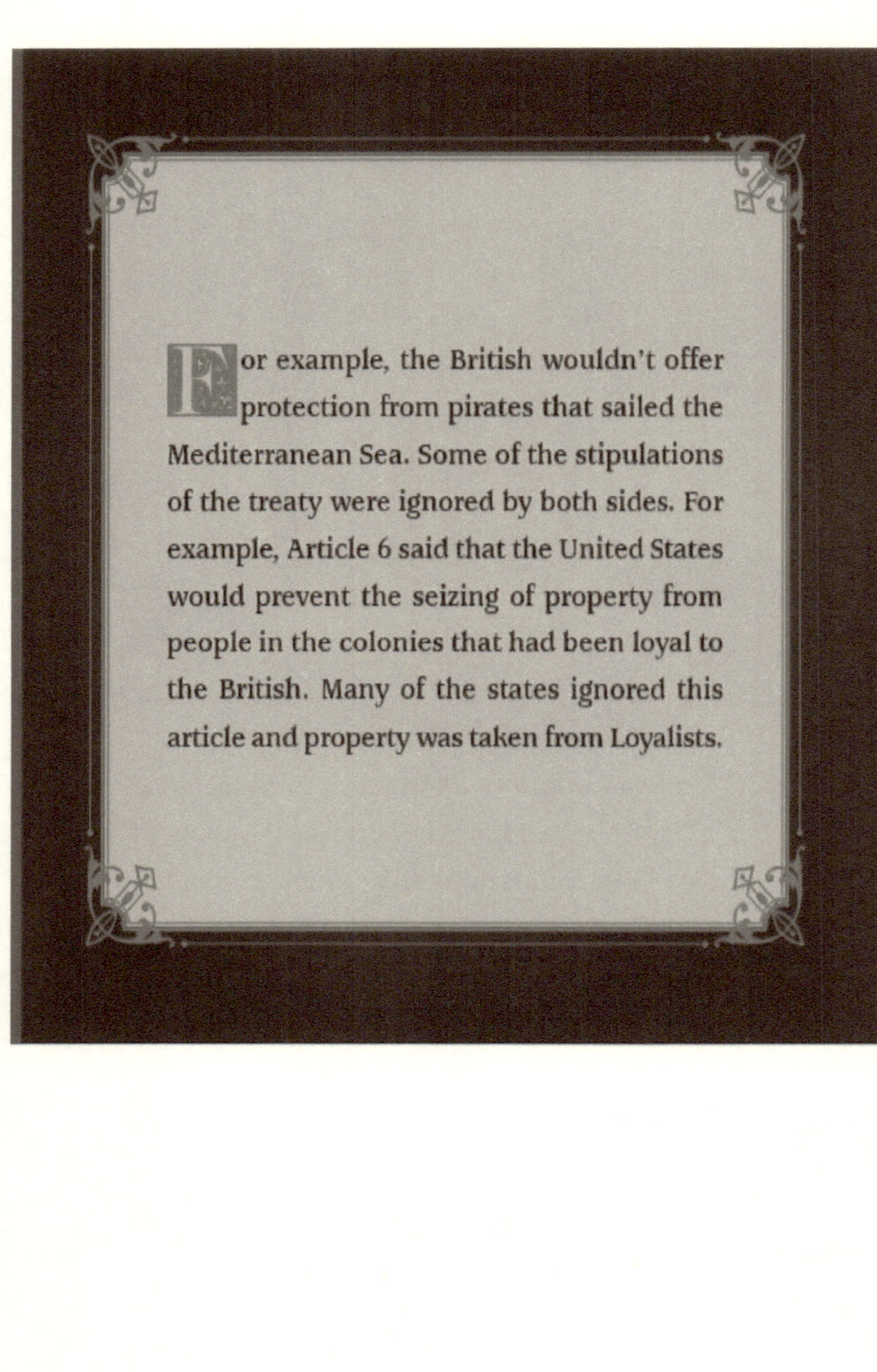

For example, the British wouldn't offer protection from pirates that sailed the Mediterranean Sea. Some of the stipulations of the treaty were ignored by both sides. For example, Article 6 said that the United States would prevent the seizing of property from people in the colonies that had been loyal to the British. Many of the states ignored this article and property was taken from Loyalists.

Article 7 stated that British slaves would remain in the United States and be given up, but the British often ignored this article. Another aspect of the treaty that the British violated was that they wouldn't occupy forts within the lands of the United States.

OHIO STATE CAPITAL
BUILDING IN COLUMBUS

SUMMARY

The American Revolutionary War had been winding down for two years before the British government and the American colonies, soon to be the United States of America, came to the bargaining table to negotiate a final treaty. The Treaty of Paris was signed on September 3, 1783 and it ended the American Revolutionary War. It was formally ratified a few months later.